W9-AET-705

DIG DEEP!

Bugs That Live Underground

Ground Beetles

Erin Long

PowerKiDS
press.

New York

Published in 2017 by The Rosen Publishing Group, Inc.
29 East 21st Street, New York, NY 10010

First Edition

Editor: Sarah Machajewski
Book Design: Mickey Harmon

Photo Credits: Cover (sky) Severe/Shutterstock.com; cover (background) ifong/ Shutterstock.com; cover (beetle) MF Photo/Shutterstock.com; pp. 3–4, 6, 8, 10, 12, 14, 16, 18, 20, 22–24 (background) isaravut/Shutterstock.com; pp. 5, 22 Henrik Larsson/Shutterstock.com; p. 7 © Santiago Urquijo/Moment Open/Getty Images; p. 9 Davit Buachidze/Shutterstock.com; p. 11 (inset) Tomatito/Shutterstock.com; p. 11 (beetle) Chris Moody/Shutterstock.com; p. 13 (pupa) https://upload.wikimedia. org/wikipedia/commons/6/64/Carabidae_pupa.jpg; p. 13 (adult beetle) Sergey Toronto/Shutterstock.com; p. 13 (eggs) pattara puttiwong/Shutterstock.com; p. 13 (larva) John Macgregor/Photolibrary/Getty Images; p. 15 Florian Andronache/ Shutterstock.com; p. 17 Nature's Images/Science Source/Getty Images; p. 19 Dan Dangler - Rochester, NY/Moment Open/Getty Images; p. 21 kingfisher/ Shutterstock.com.

Cataloging-in-Publication Data

Names: Long, Erin.
Title: Ground beetles / Erin Long.
Description: New York : PowerKids Press, 2017. | Series: Dig deep! bugs that live underground | Includes index.
Identifiers: ISBN 9781499420548 (pbk.) | ISBN 9781499420562 (library bound) | ISBN 9781499420555 (6 pack)
Subjects: LCSH: Beetles–Juvenile literature.
Classification: LCC QL576.2 L65 2017| DDC 595.76–dc23

Manufactured in the United States of America

CPSIA Compliance Information: Batch #BS16PK: For Further Information contact Rosen Publishing, New York, New York at 1-800-237-9932

Contents

Creepy Crawlers 4

One Big Family 6

Big Appetites 8

Beetle Body 10

A Life in Stages 12

New Life 14

Growing Up 16

Grown-Up Ground Beetles 18

Cool Species 20

Under the Ground 22

Glossary 23

Index 24

Websites 24

Creepy Crawlers

Millions of bugs populate the planet. These creepy, crawly creatures live in all kinds of **habitats**, from deserts and mountains to our own backyards. Many kinds of bugs live where we can't see them, including underground! Ground beetles belong to this group.

You probably don't see ground beetles too often. They're mostly active at night. Even if it doesn't seem like it, they're very common. In fact, ground beetles are one of the most common kinds of beetles in North America. Let's dig deep to find out more about this interesting **insect**.

If you're looking for ground beetles, the ground is the best place to start! →

One Big Family

Ground beetles are part of a family called Carabidae. This family is very large, with about 40,000 known **species** living around the world. However, there are probably species that haven't been discovered yet! Scientists think around 2,000 kinds of ground beetles live in North America.

Ground beetles are found in almost every habitat, especially forests and fields. They've been found living near oceans, on mountains, and in the desert. Ground beetles are most likely to be seen crawling on the ground or on logs or leaves.

Dig Deeper!

Hundreds of species of ground beetles can live in the same area.

This purple ground beetle is probably looking for food.

Big Appetites

Ground beetles play an important part in keeping Earth's habitats healthy. They eat all kinds of bugs, which keeps pest populations low.

Ground beetles are big eaters. In fact, it's said they can eat their body weight in food in one day. Some ground beetles eat specific creatures, such as caterpillars and slugs. Ground beetles may also eat ants, aphids, maggots, and worms.

Some ground beetles are also known to eat the seeds of weeds, or wild plants that grow where they're not wanted. Ground beetles are very helpful in this way!

Ground beetles are considered **beneficial** bugs, since their eating habits help their **environment**.

In general, ground beetles find their food just by coming across it. However, some species seem to hunt for their food by sight.

Beetle Body

Most adult ground beetles measure between 0.125 and 1.25 inches(0.32 and 3.18 cm). Many are shiny and black or brown. However, some species are green, yellow, orange, or purple. Some are iridescent, which means their color changes when you look at them from different angles.

Ground beetles have wing covers, which commonly have **grooves**. However, most species don't fly. Ground beetles also have antennae, or feelers, and mouthparts they use to chew their **prey**. Ground beetles have six long legs they use to run fast. They're not great climbers, which is why they're usually found near the ground.

A close-up look at a ground beetle shows its grooved wing covers, feelers, and mouthparts. Each of the beetle's body parts help it survive. →

mouthparts

feelers

legs

grooved wing
covers

A Life in Stages

All beetles, including ground beetles, go through metamorphosis. This is the process of growing from a young form to an adult form in stages. Ground beetles go through a complete metamorphosis, which means they have four separate stages in their **life cycle**. The stages are egg, **larva**, **pupa**, and adult. Big changes happen at each stage!

Adult ground beetles live between one and four years. On average, they produce one **generation** of new beetles a year. Some species lay eggs that hatch in the summer, while others lay eggs that hatch in the winter. This is just the beginning of their interesting life.

Dig Deeper!

Larger ground beetle species tend to live longer.

adult

eggs

larva

upa

The ground beetle's life cycle keeps going so long as adult ground beetles lay eggs.

New Life

Female ground beetles lay between 30 and 600 eggs at a time. They lay their eggs directly in the soil or within the plant matter that sits on top of the soil. Females must lay their eggs in a safe spot, since predators will eat the larvae if they find them.

Eggs hatch after about a week. The ground beetles are now in the larval stage. A larva's body is soft and sometimes hairy. It's usually brown or black on top and creamy white underneath. Larvae live in the soil for about a year. They're predators that eat small invertebrates and their eggs.

Ground beetles look very different in the larval stage than they do as adults!

Dig Deeper!

An invertebrate is an animal that doesn't have a backbone. Beetles are invertebrates.

Growing Up

Ground beetles live underground for the entire larval stage. They remain there until they're ready to come above ground as adults. Larvae molt several times as they grow. Molting is when an insect sheds its exoskeleton, or outer shell, and grows a new one in its place.

Before ground beetles enter the pupal stage, they go through two to four instars. Instars are periods of time between molts. When they're ready, the larvae dig deeper into the soil and enter the pupal stage. This is the stage during which beetles turn into adults. After about 5 to 10 days, they're officially done growing. They're now ready to come above ground!

Dig Deeper!

Pupae rest and stay safe in a soil chamber, or tiny pocket in the soil. This is important since pupae can't move or defend themselves against predators.

A pupa is an insect that's inactive and immature, which means it's not fully grown. Ground beetles lose their larval form and take on their adult form during this stage.

Grown-Up Ground Beetles

An adult ground beetle spends most of its life near the ground. During the day, it hides under leaves, logs, and other plant matter. Ground beetles really come to life at night. When it gets dark, they crawl out of their hiding spaces and start hunting.

Ground beetles are predators, but they have their own predators, too. However, their body has a tough shell for protection. They can also run quickly away from danger. Some species of ground beetles give off a bad smell that tells predators to stay away. Hunting at night may be the best protection, because many predators are sleeping!

Dig Deeper!

Some ground beetles' bad smell keeps birds from eating them.

This ground beetle was no match for a hungry praying mantis.

Cool Species

Some kinds of ground beetles are really interesting. A kind of beetle called a snail hunter has mouthparts in the shape of hooks. They're great for getting a snail's body out of its protective shell. Caterpillar hunters, another kind of beetle, have really bright colors—but don't get too close. They give off a liquid that can really hurt our skin.

The bombardier beetle also knows how to hurt its enemies. It can spray boiling-hot liquid at them! The beetles make a popping sound when they spray. This noise is also meant to scare the predators away. Beetles are cool!

Dig Deeper!

Ground beetles may sound scary, but they generally don't hurt people.

The bombardier beetle's unusual coloring helps it stand out.

Under the Ground

After a night of hunting, ground beetles go back to their hiding places. They rest under leaves and logs, waiting for another night to begin. When the world wakes up, ground beetles are safe and out of sight.

You may not think about ground beetles if you can't see them—but they're definitely there. They live almost everywhere. The next time you take a walk in the woods or play in your yard, try to remember what you've learned. There are probably plenty of ground beetles hiding nearby!

Glossary

beneficial: Having a good effect.

environment: The natural world in which a plant or animal lives.

generation: A group of living creatures born about the same time.

groove: A long, narrow cut.

habitat: The natural place where an animal, insect, or plant lives.

insect: A bug with six legs and one or two pairs of wings.

larva: A stage in an insect's life between the egg and the adult stages. The plural is "larvae."

life cycle: A series of changes a living creature goes through from birth to death.

pupa: A bug that is changing from a larva to adult, usually inside a case or cocoon. The plural is "pupae."

prey: An animal that is hunted by other animals for food.

species: A group of living organisms that share similar traits and that can come together to make babies.

Index

B
birds, 18
bombardier beetle, 20, 21

C
Carabidae, 6
caterpillar hunter, 20

D
deserts, 4, 6

E
eggs, 12, 13, 14
exoskeleton, 16

F
feelers, 10, 11
fields, 6
food, 7, 8, 9
forests, 6

I
instars, 16
invertebrates, 14, 15

L
larva, 12, 13, 14, 16, 17
legs, 10, 11

M
metamorphosis, 12
molt, 16
mountains, 4, 6
mouthparts, 10, 11, 20

N
North America, 4, 6

P
praying mantis, 19
predators, 14, 16, 18, 20
pupa, 12, 13, 16, 17

S
snail hunter, 20
species, 6, 9, 10, 12, 18, 20

W
wing covers, 10, 11

Websites

Due to the changing nature of Internet links, PowerKids Press has developed an online list of websites related to the subject of this book. This site is updated regularly. Please use this link to access the list: www.powerkidslinks.com/digd/beet